T·H·E B·E·S·T O·F
CHOCOLATE

T·H·E B·E·S·T O·F
CHOCOLATE

JG PRESS

4443
Published in the USA 1995 by JG Press
Distributed by World Publications, Inc.
Copyright © 1995 by CLB Publishing
Godalming, Surrey, UK

Printed and bound in Italy
ISBN 1-57215-046-7

The JG Press imprint is a trademark of JG Press, Inc.
455 Somerset Avenue
North Dighton, MA 02764

CONTENTS

INTRODUCTION

Chocolate is a universal favorite, associated with indulgences and romance around the world. Ancient Mexican Aztecs are credited with its discovery, and their influence is still seen today in the use of chocolate in savory Mexican and Latin dishes.

This luscious confection is made from cocoa beans with varying amounts of sugar and fat, and comes in a wide range of colors and flavors. Milk chocolate, as its name implies, has had milk added during production. Semi-sweet chocolate is lighter and has less sugar than the darker bitter sweet variety. For fine and delicate candies buy couverture or coating chocolate, available for some of the larger supermarkets. Avoid chocolate-flavored cake covering for all the recipes in this book; it is not a true chocolate.

Chocolate's link with romance was probably established because it contains caffeine, which gives a quick burst of energy, as well as a natural amphetamine called phenylethylamine. Scientists say our brain produces this chemical in varying amounts, and if our body contains more than normal levels we experience rapidly changing emotions . . . just like being in love!

Dieters are well aware of the high calories in chocolate: plain chocolate has 525 per 4 oz, while milk chocolate has 530 for the same amount. Yet, there are a few nutritional benefits to chocolate, as it contains small amounts of protein, carbohydrate, iron, potassium and calcium. In fact, a 4 oz bar of milk chocolate contains almost half the daily recommended amount of calcium for grown-ups.

Carob, made from the pod of a tree often grown in the Mediterranean, is a popular health-food alternative to chocolate because it does not contain caffeine. Buy it in bar form from health food shops and be sure to read the label because it is often flavored rather than plain.

Take great care when melting chocolate because it can easily burn. All the recipes in this book recommend either melting the chocolate in a liquid, or melting it in a bowl over simmering water.

CHURROS Y CHOCOLATE

3½ cups flour
1¼ cups milk
1¼ cups water
2 eggs, beaten
Extra virgin olive oil
Sugar for dusting

Hot chocolate
6 oz bittersweet chocolate
1¼ cups milk, boiling

Start by preparing the hot chocolate. Break chocolate into small pieces and place these in a double boiler, or a heat-proof bowl that will fit snugly over a pan of simmering water. Fit bowl over simmering water and melt chocolate. As the chocolate begins to melt, stir in a little of the boiling milk until smooth and thick. Stir in the remaining milk, stirring constantly. Keep warm.

Sift flour on to a piece of wax paper. Place milk and water in a saucepan and bring to boiling point. Tip in flour all at once, then stir until it forms a ball and comes away from the sides of the pan. Take pan off heat. Add eggs, stirring all the time until mixture is smooth.

In a thick-bottomed saucepan, heat olive oil until it begins to smoke. Fill a pastry bag fitted with a large round nozzle with churros dough. Squeeze long strips of dough into olive oil and fry until they are golden. With a slotted spoon, remove churros from oil and pat with kitchen paper to absorb excess oil. Dust with sugar and keep warm. To serve, pour hot chocolate into 2 warm mugs. Dunk churros into hot chocolate and eat.

This is a popular Spanish breakfast dish.

Serves 2

MEXICAN CHICKEN MOLA

1 roasting chicken, 2½–3 lbs
1 carrot, chopped
1 onion, chopped
2 celery stalks, chopped
1 bay leaf
Salt
Water

Mola sauce
1 onion, chopped
2 cloves garlic, finely crushed
2 small hot green chilies, seeded and chopped
¾ cup blanched almonds, chopped
¼ cup seedless raisins
½ teaspoon coriander seeds
¼ teaspoon ground aniseed
1 slice toast
2 large tomatoes, stems removed
2–3 sprigs fresh coriander
½ teaspoon ground cinnamon
1 tablespoon lard
1½ squares unsweetened chocolate, grated
Salt and black pepper

Quarter chicken, carefully removing any lumps of fat from body cavity. Put chicken pieces in a pan with carrot, onion, celery stalks, bay leaf and just enough salted water to cover and cook gently, covered, until tender. This will take about 45 minutes.

Drain chicken pieces, reserving cooking liquor. Keep hot. Strain cooking liquor and reserve ⅔ cup.

In an electric blender or food processor, combine onion, chilies, almonds, raisins, coriander seeds, aniseed, toast, tomatoes, coriander and cinnamon. Process to a purée.

In a large frying pan, heat the lard. Add purée and cook for 5 minutes, stirring all the time. Stir in reserved cooking liquor, chocolate, and salt and pepper to taste, stirring until chocolate has melted.

Return chicken pieces to pan and bring to simmering point. Cook gently, covered, 15–20 minutes longer. Serve immediately.

Serves 4

CORNISH HENS IN CHOCOLATE

4 oven-ready Cornish hens
Salt and black pepper
⅔ cup flour
¼ cup extra virgin olive oil
16 pickling onions, peeled
3 cloves garlic, finely sliced
3 tablespoons dry white wine
⅓ cup chicken or game stock
1½ oz bittersweet chocolate, finely grated
Lemon wedges, for garnish

Wipe the hens with a damp cloth and season them inside and out with salt and black pepper. Place ½ cup flour in a polythene bag and add the hens one by one. Shake the bag until each hen is well coated. Remove from the bag and shake off any excess.

In a heavy, flameproof casserole wide enough to take all the hens in one layer, heat olive oil, and brown birds on all sides. With a slotted spoon, take birds out of casserole. Add onions to casserole and push them around until they are browned on all sides. With a slotted spoon, take onions out of casserole.

Add garlic to casserole, and cook over a high heat for 1–2 minutes. Stir in remaining flour and cook for about 2 minutes. Add wine and stock and bring to boiling point, stirring constantly until the stock thickens.
Return hens to casserole and cover tightly. Simmer over a low heat for about 40 minutes. Add onions and salt and pepper to taste. Cover again and continue simmering for about 15 minutes until birds are cooked through.
Transfer hens and onions to a heated serving platter and keep hot. Skim any fat from cooking liquor in casserole. Stir in chocolate, and simmer, stirring until melted. Spoon sauce over hens and garnish platter with lemon wedges. Serve immediately.

Serves 4

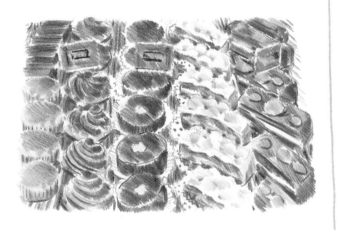

FRUITY FONDUE

8 oz bittersweet chocolate
⅔ cup heavy cream
Pinch of grated nutmeg
½ teaspoon ground cloves
½ teaspoon ground cinnamon
Pinch of ground mixed spice
4 tablespoons Tia Maria, dark rum or brandy
Mixed fresh fruit pieces, to serve

Break chocolate into small pieces and place these in a fondue pot over a heat source. Add cream. Stir until chocolate and cream are thick and smooth. Stir in grated nutmeg, ground cloves, ground cinnamon and mixed spice, then stir in liqueur.

Keep sauce bubbling over a heat source. Serve with banana chunks, pineapple pieces, orange wedges and strawberries. Spear fruit with long-handled forks and dip in hot fondue sauce.

Serves 4

POIRES BELLE HÉLÈNE

6 juicy pears, peeled, halved, cored, poached and chilled
6 scoops vanilla ice cream

Bittersweet chocolate sauce
6 oz bittersweet chocolate
2 tablespoons butter
⅔ cup heavy cream
Vanilla extract, to taste

Start by preparing the sauce. Break chocolate into top of a double boiler. Add butter and stir over simmering water until chocolate and butter are smooth. Beat in cream a little at a time. Place top part of pan over direct heat, bring sauce to boiling point, stirring all the time, and simmer, stirring, for 2–3 minutes. Remove from heat and flavor with a few drops of vanilla.

Drain pears and lightly pat them dry with kitchen paper. Put a scoop of ice cream in each of 6 glass dishes. Press half a pear to opposite sides of each scoop of ice cream, pointed ends up, and mask with warm chocolate sauce. Serve immediately.

Serves 6

CHOCOLATE-ORANGE MOUSSE

4 oz bittersweet chocolate
2 tablespoons butter
Finely grated rind and juice of 1 orange
1 tablespoon orange-flavored liqueur
2 eggs, separated

Break chocolate into small pieces and place these in a heat-proof bowl that will fit snugly over a pan of simmering water. Add butter and orange rind and juice. Use a double boiler, or fit bowl over simmering water and melt chocolate and butter. Cool slightly and stir in orange liqueur.

In a bowl, whisk egg yolks until fluffy. Pour in chocolate mixture, whisking all the time. Whisk egg whites until stiff but not dry and fold into the chocolate mixture. Pour into 4 individual soufflé dishes; allow to become quite cold and chill until ready to serve.

Serves 4

HOT SOUFFLÉ

Butter and extra sugar for soufflé dish
¼ cup sugar
3 oz bittersweet chocolate
4 tablespoons brandy
3 tablespoons butter
2 tablespoons flour
⅔ cup milk
3 eggs, separated
1 extra egg white
Cocoa powder, for dusting

Start by preparing soufflé dish. Grease bottom and insides of a 4-cup soufflé dish. Coat insides of dish with sugar, then tip out excess.

Break chocolate into small pieces and place in a small double boiler, or in a heat-proof bowl that will fit snugly over a pan of simmering water. Place over simmering water and melt chocolate. Remove from heat, and stir in brandy.

Melt butter in a saucepan and stir in flour. Cook for 2 minutes, stirring all the time. Remove from heat, stir in milk, then bring to boiling point and simmer for 2 minutes, stirring until thick.

Remove pan from heat and stir in sugar, melted chocolate and egg yolks.

In a large bowl, beat egg whites until stiff but not dry. Using a large metal spoon, carefully fold egg whites into chocolate mixture. Spoon mixture into soufflé dish. Bake soufflé in moderately hot oven 400°F, for 35 minutes or until well risen. Remove from oven and quickly sift cocoa powder over top. Serve immediately.

Serves 4

THE QUEEN'S BAVAROIS

2 teaspoons unflavored powdered gelatin
¼ cup sugar
2 eggs, separated
1¼ cups milk
2 oz bittersweet chocolate
⅔ cup heavy cream
Chocolate sprinkles and whipped cream for decoration

Sprinkle gelatin over 3 tablespoons cold water in a small cup. Then, when the gelatin has absorbed the water and set, stand the cup in a pan of hot water, stirring until the liquid is clear. Allow to cool to room temperature.

In a large double boiler, or a heat-proof bowl that will fit snugly over a pan of simmering water, whisk the egg yolks and sugar together until light, fluffy and almost white. Put milk and chocolate in a thick-bottomed saucepan and bring to boiling point, stirring until chocolate is melted. Off the heat, pour gradually into the egg yolks and sugar, whisking all the time. Fit bowl

over simmering water and cook, stirring until custard is
thick enough to coat back of spoon. Take care not to let
it boil, or egg yolks will curdle.

Remove from heat and stir in a gelatin mixture. Pour
through a strainer into a clean bowl. Leave until quite
cold, stirring occasionally.

Whisk egg whites to a firm snow. In another bowl,
whisk cream until thick and floppy but not stiff. With a
large metal spoon, fold cream into chocolate mixture,
followed by egg whites. Spoon into a well-greased
mold. Chill for several hours in refrigerator.

Serve unmolded and decorated with whipped cream
and chocolate sprinkles.

Serves 6–8

TRUFFLE AND HAZELNUT RING

3¼ cups light cream
1 scant cup sugar
7 egg yolks, lightly beaten
1 scant cup cocoa powder
¾ cup heavy cream
6 oz bittersweet chocolate, chopped
6 tablespoons any nut liqueur
2 tablespoons orange-flavored liqueur
½ cup toasted hazelnuts, chopped
Whipped cream and chocolate curls, for decoration

In a thick-bottomed saucepan, gently heat cream and sugar together, stirring until sugar dissolves. Bring almost to boiling point, then take off heat and allow to cool for 5 minutes.

Place eggs in a large bowl and gradually pour cream on to eggs, whisking all the time. Strain mixture into rinsed-out saucepan and heat very gently over low heat, until custard is creamy and stays separated if you run your finger through it on the back of a wooden spoon. Take care not to let it boil, or egg yolks will curdle. Take off heat and stir in cocoa. Leave until quite cold, stirring occasionally. Pour custard into a freezer-proof container, cover and freeze until solid around edges.

Place heavy cream and chocolate in a small saucepan over low heat, stirring until chocolate melts. Take off heat and stir in liqueurs and hazelnuts. Allow to cool completely.

Line bottom of a 6-cup ring mold with three-quarters of chocolate ice cream. With a small spoon, push ice cream up sides of mold to form a deep groove in centre. Place in freezer for a few minutes to firm. Pour cream and hazelnut mixture into groove, then cover with remaining ice cream. Cover and freeze until firm.

Transfer to the main compartment of refrigerator about 30 minutes before serving. Unmold and decorate with whipped cream and chocolate curls just before serving.

Serves 8–10

MINTY CHOCOLATE ICE CREAM

¼ cup sugar
3 egg yolks
1¼ cups light cream
1¼ cups heavy cream
8 tablespoons crème de menthe
4 oz bittersweet chocolate, coarsely chopped

In a thick-bottomed saucepan, dissolve the sugar in ½ cup water. Place a sugar thermometer in the water. Bring to boiling point and boil until a temperature of 194°F is reached.

In a large bowl, beat egg yolks. Pour sugar syrup on to egg yolks, beating all the time until mixture is thick and light. In another large bowl, beat creams together until soft peaks form. With a large metal spoon, fold into the egg yolk mixture, followed by crème de menthe and chocolate pieces.

Transfer to an ice cube tray or shallow plastic box. Cover and freeze until firm. Transfer to the main compartment of refrigerator about 30 minutes before serving.

Serves 6

DOUBLE CHOCOLATE CHIP COOKIES

¾ cup butter, room temperature
Scant ½ cup sugar
Generous 1 cup soft brown sugar
1 teaspoon vanilla extract
2 egg, lightly beaten
1¾ cups flour
2 tablespoons cocoa powder
1 teaspoon bicarbonate of soda
1 teaspoon salt
1¼ cups chocolate chips
Butter for baking sheet

Cream butter, sugar, brown sugar and vanilla extract together until light and fluffy. Add eggs and beat well. Sift flour, cocoa powder, bicarbonate of soda and salt together on to the creamed mixture. Beat together, then beat in chocolate chips.

Drop the mixture in well-spaced mounds on a buttered baking sheet. Bake in a moderate oven 375°F, for 8–10 minutes, until cookies are firm to the touch. (You will have to bake in several batches.) Allow to cool on baking sheet for a few minutes, then use a round-bladed knife to transfer to a rack to cool. Store in an air-tight container.

Makes about 60 cookies

TRADITIONAL BROWNIES

4 oz bittersweet chocolate
½ cup cold butter, diced
⅔ cup soft brown sugar
1 cup flour
Pinch of salt
2 eggs, lightly beaten
Generous ½ cup walnuts, chopped
2 tablespoons milk
Butter for cake pan

Break chocolate into small pieces and place these in a
double boiler, or a heat-proof bowl that will fit snugly
over a pan of simmering water. Add butter. Fit bowl
over simmering water and melt chocolate and butter.
Stir until smooth. Remove from heat. Stir in sugar and
beat until well combined. Allow to cool.

Sift flour and salt into a bowl, and make a well in the center. Pour in cooled chocolate. Beat, gradually drawing in flour from the sides. Beat in eggs, walnuts and milk to make a soft dropping consistency.

Pour into a well-buttered 8 in square cake pan. Bake in a moderate oven 350°F for 30 minutes until a skewer pushed right down to the bottom through the middle comes out clean and dry. Allow brownies to cool in pan before cutting into 16 squares.

Makes 16

DARK DATE CAKE

4½ tablespoons flour
3 tablespoons unsweetened cocoa powder
1 teaspoon baking powder
4 eggs, separated
1 cup sugar
2-3 tablespoons fresh orange juice
⅔ cup stoned dried dates, chopped
⅔ cup walnuts, chopped
Pinch of salt
Butter for cake pan
1¼ cups heavy cream

Sift flour with cocoa and baking powder. Beat egg yolks and sugar together until thick and fluffy. Beat in 2 tablespoons orange juice. Sift flour and cocoa mixture again over the surface, and with a large metal spoon, lightly fold it in, together with a little more orange juice if necessary to make a light, creamy batter. Fold in chopped dates and walnuts until mixed.

Beat egg whites with a pinch of salt until stiff but not dry. Gently fold into cake batter. Immediately spoon batter into a well-buttered 9 in tube pan. Bake in a slow oven 325°F until cake is well risen, lightly colored on top and has shrunk away slightly from sides of tin. This will take 35–40 minutes.

Allow cake to 'settle' for 15 minutes before turning out on a wire rack. Leave until quite cold before covering with lightly sweetened whipped cream.

Serves 6–8

CITRUS PECAN CAKE

1 scant cup pecans, finely ground
4 tablespoons flour
1 tablespoon baking powder
Generous pinch of salt
Finely grated rind of 1 orange
Juice of ½ orange
4 eggs, separated
⅔ cup sugar
4 tablespoons melted butter
Pecan halves, to decorate

Chocolate icing
4 oz bittersweet chocolate
3 tablespoons melted butter

Mix the ground nuts with the flour, baking powder, salt and orange rind. Beat the egg yolks until thick and lemon-colored, then gradually beat in half the sugar.

Fold in walnut mixture, followed by orange juice. Whisk egg whites until they form soft, floppy peaks. Gradually add remaining sugar, whisking constantly to make a stiff meringue. Fold meringue into yolk mixture.

Spoon cake mixture into a well-buttered, deep 8 in cake pan. Bake in a moderate oven 350°F for 40 minutes. Allow cake to cool in its pan on a rack for 10 minutes before turning it out on to the rack and leaving it until cold.

To make chocolate icing, break the chocolate into small pieces and place these in a double boiler or in a heat-proof bowl that will fit snugly over a pan of simmering water and leave until chocolate has melted, stirring frequently. Stir in butter and beat until smooth. Spread icing over cake top and sides. Decorate with pecan halves.

Serves 4–6

CAROB CREATIONS

¾ cup carob flour
¼ cup butter
⅔ cup brown sugar
¾ cup flour
½ teaspoon baking powder
1 egg, beaten
1 teaspoon vanilla extract
½ teaspoon salt
¼ cup walnut halves, chopped
Butter for cake pan

Sift carob into the top of a double boiler, or in a heat-proof bowl that will fit snugly over a pan of simmering water with 2 tablespoons of water, butter and sugar. Fit bowl over simmering water and melt. Take off heat.
Sift flour and baking powder on to melted chocolate mixture. Add remaining ingredients and mix well.
Spoon into a well-buttered 8 in square cake pan. Bake in a moderate oven 350°F for 15 minutes until slightly risen and shiny on top. Allow to cool in pan.
To serve, cut into bars. Store in an airtight container.

Makes 16 bars

STRAWBERRY QUAKE

2 lbs strawberries, hulled and puréed
3 cups sugar
Butter for baking sheet
1 lb coating chocolate

Place strawberry purée in a thick-bottomed saucepan. Stir in sugar. Cook over a low heat, stirring all the time until mixture is thick enough for a clean line to be left on bottom of pan when a spoon is drawn across it. Remove pan from heat.

Distribute mixture in about 24 little mounds on a well-buttered baking sheet. Leave to set.

When each strawberry jelly is firm to touch, prepare the chocolate coating. Break chocolate into small pieces and place in small heat-proof bowl that will fit snugly over a pan of simmering water. Place over simmering water and melt chocolate. Beat until smooth and creamy. Place a sugar thermometer in the chocolate and leave until temperature has fallen to 110°F.

Line a baking sheet with wax paper. Drop jellies, one at a time, into chocolate. Lift out with a fork and slide on to baking sheet. Leave for several hours until chocolate is completely hard. Store between pieces of wax paper in an airtight container.

Makes about 24

CARNIVAL IN RIO

3 cups Brazil nuts, shelled
1 lb coating chocolate

Put the nuts on a baking tray and roast in a slow oven 325°F until the skins become flaky. Peel off skins, wash nuts and dry on kitchen paper. Break chocolate into small pieces and place these in a heat-proof bowl that will fit snugly over a pan of simmering water. Fit bowl over simmering water and melt chocolate. Use a sugar thermometer to check the temperature of the chocolate. It should never exceed 120°F. When the chocolate has melted completely, stir until the consistency is creamy and smooth.

Place the sugar thermometer in the chocolate and leave until the temperature has fallen to 110°F. Place the nuts on a sheet by the side of the bowl. Line another sheet with wax paper. Drop one nut at a time into the melted chocolate. Lift out on a fork, tapping the fork on the side of the bowl to remove excess chocolate. Slide chocolate Brazil nuts on to lined sheet. Leave for about an hour, until the chocolate is completely hard, before eating.

Makes 1 lb

ITALIAN GAME SAUCE

3 tablespoons brown sugar
5 tablespoons currants
4 oz bittersweet chocolate, grated
1 tablespoon chopped candied orange peel
1 tablespoon chopped candied lemon peel
1 cup red wine vinegar
1 tablespoon capers
1 tablespoon pine nuts

Place brown sugar, currants, grated chocolate, candied orange and lemon peels, red wine vinegar and capers in a saucepan. Allow to soak for 2 hours.
Simmer sauce for 2 minutes, stirring occasionally. Stir in pine nuts just before serving. Serve with game, grilled turkey drumsticks or duck.

Serves 4

RICH FUDGE SAUCE

4 oz bittersweet chocolate
½ cup cold butter, diced
⅔ cup soft brown sugar
½ cup sugar
1¼ cups evaporated milk

Break chocolate into a thick-bottomed saucepan. Add butter and all the sugars. Place pan over medium heat and stir until chocolate is melted and sugars dissolved. Stir in milk. Bring sauce to boiling point, stirring constantly, and simmer, stirring, for 5 minutes. Remove from heat.

Serve sauce hot or warm with ice creams, frozen yogurts, pancakes or hot puddings.

Serves 4

BUTTERCREAM ICING

4 oz bittersweet chocolate
4 egg yolks
½ cup sugar
1 cup butter, room temperature
2–3 teaspoons vanilla extract

Break chocolate into small pieces and place these in a double boiler, or heat-proof bowl that will fit snugly over a pan of simmering water. Fit bowl over simmering water and melt chocolate, stirring until smooth. Remove from heat and allow to cool until just beginning to set.

Whisk egg yolks. In thick-bottomed saucepan, heat sugar gently with 7 tablespoons of water, stirring until dissolved. Bring to boiling point. Use a sugar thermometer to check the temperature of syrup. It should reach 240°F. Remove from heat.

Whisking constantly, pour syrup on to egg yolks in steady stream. Whisk until cool, pale and mousse-like. Cream butter until it is same consistency as yolk mixture. Beat it gradually into yolks. Stir in cooled chocolate and vanilla.

CAROB SMOOTHIE

5 cups milk
3 tablespoons molasses
3 tablespoons carob flour
1 ripe banana, peeled
⅓ cup shelled peanuts, finely ground

Put all the ingredients in an electric blender or food processor and whirl until smooth and creamy. Serve in tall, chilled glasses.

Serves 4